How College Students Manage Their Time

Table of Contents

Pg. 3	Welcome to College!
Pg. 4	Setting Goals
Pg. 7	Time is On Your Side (Tracking Your Time)
Pg. 10	Your Planner is Your Friend (Using a Daily Planner)
Pg. 16	Time Management 101
Pg. 22	Now Where Did I Put That? (Organization Skills)
Pg. 26	I'll Stop Procrastinating Tomorrow
Pg. 31	AAAAHHHH! (Stress Management)
Pg. 41	Stop The Cramming! (Study Tips)
Pg. 46	Workin 9 to 5 (Managing Work and Studies)
Pg. 50	Just Because There's Checks In The Book (Money Management)
Pg. 54	Party Responsibly
Pg. 57	But I'm Not 18 Anymore! (Non-traditional Students)
Pg. 59	You Can Do It!!!

WELCOME TO COLLEGE!

You've walked across the stage, collected your diploma and spent a summer dreaming of the freedom you'll enjoy in college! Congratulations! You're embarking on a journey sure to be filled with fun, new friends, new experiences, and knowledge beyond your dreams.

Some questions you might be asking yourself include:

1. How do I get everything done I need to get done?
2. How do I fit all MY stuff in the room with ALL my roommate's stuff?
3. Where's the cafeteria?
4. Where's the party?

While all of these questions are of extreme importance, the one you need to focus on the most is the first one.

At first, you will have more time available to you now than you will know what to do with. Even if you take a huge class load, run a marathon a day, start a quilting bee, and even sleep, I guarantee that you are going to have more time than you can really believe. It's maximizing that time that makes all the difference in succeeding in college or struggling.

For many college freshmen, this experience can be a difficult transition. Your parents aren't around anymore to make sure you get up for school. You go from being a "big" senior to a "greenie" freshman again. College is more than just an excuse to party. It's a beginning for your adult life. You will be learning what you need to know to succeed in the real world. That, alone, can be overwhelming!

But it doesn't have to be. All you need to do is learn time management skills along with ways to cope with stress and maximize your college experience. How do you do that? It's not always easy, but it can be easier – with the help of this valuable guide.

Inside these pages are valuable tips to learn how to schedule your time effectively, how to stop procrastinating, how to shut out distractions, and how to manage your studies and work with your personal life. A huge part of this experience is stress management, and we've provided many valuable tips and tricks to minimize stress and enjoy the whole college experience.

We all probably wish that there were more hours in a day, but since that is impossible, we must make the best use of the hours that we do have. By utilizing the tips in this book, you will be on your way to achieving better time management skills and becoming an all-around better college student.

It doesn't matter if you're an 18 year old freshman right out of high school, a senior almost ready to graduate, or a 40 year old returning to classes for the first time in 20 years, these tips can apply to everyone. And, they will apply to your life after college as well! Learning effective time management skills makes life much easier and allows you more and more time for yourself, which is as equally important.

You deserve to enjoy everything about college life - the parties, the camaraderie, the fun. You can accomplish this and not sacrifice the real reason why you're here – for an education. We can show you how!

Goal Setting

What are your goals? Really, what are your goals? Do you want to lose 10 pounds, have shinier hair, land that cute guy in your Algebra class, or get an "A" in basket weaving? Goals are important for everyone and identifying them up front helps you keep your eye on the prize.

Why set goals? Life is tremendously varied. At any given moment, there are thousands of things you could do. When you're driving, you could turn left, turn right, speed up, slam on the brakes, stop for lunch, stop for gas, decide to drive to Alaska to see what Kodiak bears look like, and on and on. But what is it that keeps you from ending up in Alaska every time you get into your car? Why don't you end up at random locations all the time? The answer is that you got into your car with a clear idea of where you wanted to go. You knew at the beginning.

Life is the same way. If you know at the beginning where you want to go, you'll probably get there. Even if detours and delays arise, eventually you'll get there. But if you don't know where you're going, you probably won't get there.

It might help to divide your goals into time frames (immediate goals, short-mid-term goals, and long-range goals). You don't have to have firm answers to those gripping questions about what you want to be or do when you're done at college to make this work; your goals are likely to shift and change over time anyway. All you need to do right now is think of a handful of goals to get started. Write down a list of goals now before reading further.

Take a look at your list of goals. How many of the tasks you intend to do today contribute to accomplishing the goals you have set for yourself? Are you actively working on these goals? Are you putting any of them off for a later time? What would you have to change in your life to make it possible to work on these goals?

Sub-dividing those goals into manageable pieces can help. Once you have a set of goals, it is useful to decompose the goals into manageable steps or sub-goals. Decomposing your goals makes it possible to tackle them one small step at a time and to reduce procrastination.

Consider for instance the goal of obtaining your degree. This goal can be broken down into four sub-goals. Each sub-goal is the successful completion of one year of your program. These sub-goals can be further broken down into individual courses within each year. The courses can be broken down into tests, exams, term papers and such within the course or into the 13 weeks of classes in each term. Each week can be further subdivided into days, and each day can be thought of in terms of the hours and minutes you'll spend in your classes and doing homework for today.

While it may seem challenging to take in the whole scope of that convergent goal, thinking of your goals in this way helps to reinforce the idea that there is a connected path linking what actions you take today and the successful completion of your goals. Seeing these connections can help you monitor your own progress and detect whether you are on track or not. Take some time now to think through the goals you've set and to break them down into their smaller constituent parts.

Now that you have a list of goals, pre-experience them in your mind. Visualizing the steps you will take to obtain the goal increases the probability of actually reaching it. Successful athletes pre-experience over and over in their minds how they are going to perform in a game so they can be at their peak effectiveness once the game begins.

One mistake made in seeking a goal is to focus so much on reaching the goal that we fail to enjoy the process of getting to it. We enjoy life more when we find satisfaction in our immediate efforts rather than thinking how nice it is going to be when we finally arrive at our distant goal.

For example, we enjoy a trip more if we decide to take an interest in the landmarks along the way rather than just enduring the ride until we arrive at our destination. Similarly, we enjoy a class more if we explore the content beyond what is required rather than just do the bare minimum to pass the class.

Don't make the mistake of setting unrealistic goals or having so many that it is impossible to reach them. We frequently do this at the beginning of the semester. We soon become discouraged when we realize we have neither the time nor the energy to accomplish all of our goals. Recognizing our physical, mental and emotional limits is an important component to realistic goal setting.

Now that you have your goals in mind, the next step is walking the road toward achieving them. That begins with time. Let's explore how to become aware of the time you have available to you

TIME IS ON YOUR SIDE

It will help you manage your time well if you know where your time actually gets spent. One very helpful way of determining your actual usage of time is to track your time. The process here is like making a schedule, but it works in reverse. Instead of writing things in that you are planning to do, time logging is a process of writing down the things that you have already done. Doing this is sort of a get-to-know-yourself exercise because this procedure will highlight many of your habits that you might selectively ignore currently.

For instance, some people find that every time they plan to do math homework they end up watching television. Instead of studying for that Psych test, they play Internet poker. Other people just can't seem to follow their schedule until the week before finals.

Whatever your time habits, time tracking will help you adjust and fine-tune your time management practices. Having accurate information about your time usage patterns can serve as another important point of reference for self-monitoring. Following are a few ways to track your time. Take a moment to do this – it will truly help you open your eyes and take control of your time.

1. Time tracking is fairly straightforward. At the end of every hour jot yourself a quick note about how you actually spent your time for that hour. The note needn't be long - one sentence or less should suffice. If how you spent your time doesn't match an already planned activity, simply enter a comment as to what you really did during that time. This way you will be able to review patterns that emerge in your use of time and make adjustments to improve your productivity.

2. Some people find it helpful to modify the planning page to facilitate tracking time. The modifications are easy enough: make two columns on your paper for each day of the week. In one column, write down the plan you are trying to follow; in the second column, make notes on what you actually did with your time. The side-by-side comparison is very telling and an excellent way to figure our where you're not using time in the way you intend.

3. Another effective way to make changes and get results from your time management strategies is to summarize your time use by time category such as: sleep, study, work, travel and so on.

   Before doing the summary, make a sheet with different columns for each category. Your log sheet might look something like this:

Activity	Expected Time	Actual Time

   Estimate the amount of time that you think you spend on the various activities listed and enter these in the "expected" row of the summary sheet. Feel free to add any additional categories that might be helpful. Then log your time for one week on an hour by hour basis. When the week is over summarize your time by category for each day, add up the values for all seven days of the week, and write the totals in the "actual" row of the summary sheet.

   Summarizing your time use allows you to understand how much time you really spend in the various areas of your life. It is almost certain that you will see a notable difference between the number of hours you expected to use in certain categories and the actual number of hours you spend.

   If you find that you spend more time in one area than you wanted, and less in another, the weekly summary of time use clearly indicates which activities to reduce to find the extra time you want for that neglected area of your life.

However you choose to understand the differences between your expected use of time and your actual use of time, your focus should be on trying to detect and adjust patterns in your own real use of time that spell trouble for you reaching your goals.

For those of you freaked out by knowing exactly where you spend your time because it only seems to reinforce your sense of time pressure, here's something to think about. We have 168 hours available in a week. Various published reports and informal studies report that fully half of those 168 hours – 84 hours - are used up for the "basics" like sleeping, eating, washing, etc. How do your own numbers compare? How will you spend the remaining 84 hours per week?

One valuable component of a time management program involves the use of a planner. Let's explore that next.

YOUR PLANNER IS YOUR BEST FRIEND

When you are organized, that will help you achieve your goals in a timely manner. You need to organize your tasks so you will know what needs to be accomplished and when they need to be accomplished. No student should be without a daily planner.

You have probably used various kinds of planning tools before, including a daily or weekly planner, a month-at-a-glance planner, and so on. It is important to keep in mind that the purpose of scheduling is not to enslave you to your planner, but rather to record your decisions about when certain things should happen.

Planners can be found in many places and in many different formats. Most college students find that a daily, week-at-a-glance planner works best as it is easier to see information for a whole week and gives plenty of room to track what needs to be done that week. Check your campus bookstore or local discount store for a variety to choose from. You can even make your own with the help of Microsoft Word or Excel. Below is an example of a sample planner page created in Excel:

March 13 - Monday	**March 16 - Thursday**
March 14 - Tuesday	**March 17 - Friday**

March 15 - Wednesday	March 18/19 - Saturday/Sunday

    Your planner should include your schedule for classes, study time, social events, club meetings, exercise time, and any other time necessary to achieve your goals. Keep the planner with you during class and note all assignments along with the due dates of those assignments. Check them off as you complete them so you know where you are at all times with your projects.

    Refer to your planner often – multiple times a day. Make this a regular part of your routine. When you get up in the morning, look at your planner to see what needs to be done for that day.

    If you have an appointment, be sure to include a phone number next to the notation in case you have to cancel or change times.

    Use a highlighter. Color-coding can help differentiate between appointments and assignments. For example, highlight in blue your classes, yellow for assignments, and green for everything else. The key here is easy recognition. When you open your planner, you can easily see what needs to be done.

Keep your planner in one specific place. Organizing your time with a calendar depends on always being able to easily put your hands on this guide. Keep it in your backpack or by your bedside table. If you use your computer a lot, keep it beside the computer when it's not in your backpack or purse.

Write due dates, and then a few days before the assignments are due, write yourself a reminder. This is especially important for large tasks that take more than a few hours to complete.

Abide by this calendar every week so you will develop a regular routine while learning how to manage your time.

The planner can be used as a time-bound memory aid, tracking major deadlines and exam dates, appointments, important anniversaries, birthdays, holidays, vacations and so on. But, you can get more out of your planner if you use it to record interim deadlines and forecast upcoming busy periods as final deadlines approach. A properly completed planner will indicate upcoming busy periods, show whether there is room in the plan for new tasks, and help you assess whether you are on target to achieve your goals.

Let's say for example that you had an upcoming exam in your Introductory Microeconomics class. Start by entering the date of the exam so you don't forget it. Next, think of the tasks that comprise the goal of doing well in the exam, think about how long each step of the task should take, and enter a series of interim deadlines for each step between the start of your preparation for the exam and the exam date itself. Use these interim deadlines as milestones to indicate the progress of your study.

If to-do lists govern your current approach to time management, then you'll be interested in the weekly objectives list. Think of the weekly objectives list as a muscle-bound to-do list. In essence, the weekly objective list is a to-do list with additional features to further decompose tasks into smaller units and to record time estimates for the task.

Let's say for example that one of your goals for the year was to maintain your honors standing and that you had a series of exams coming up including one for first year Introductory Microeconomics. You might set an objective to score a B+ or A grade on the exam and list this on your objectives list. Your next step would then be to consider a variety of study activities that would prepare you well for the examination.

You might begin by entering your first activity, "complete readings and review lecture notes", in the activities column. Once you have entered your activity it is important to assign it a time estimate. This block of time reflects an important principle in time estimating; when estimating time you might want to add time to the amount of time you think it will take you to complete the task. Refine your estimates on the basis of your experience with similar tasks.

This is important because we tend to estimate without considering possible difficulties or interruptions. Once you have entered the first activity for study, you would continue with the others you have in mind. The final two columns on the form allow you to track whether or not you have scheduled and completed the activities you have listed. Your next step is to carry the listed activities, along with their associated time estimates, to your weekly planner to be scheduled.

Take a look at your weekly planner. What do you have written in it? Likely, you list lecture times, tutorial times, laboratory times, times for extracurricular activities, and various other appointments.

If this sounds like your schedule then you are probably under-using another very versatile time management tool because many of the most important tasks (homework activities that move you toward your goals) are left out of the picture. The implication of this should be clear: If it isn't on the schedule it won't get done.

Stepping from the weekly objectives list to the weekly planner is easy. Using the time estimates for the activities on the weekly objectives list as guides find a block of time of appropriate duration in your schedule. Then write in the activities one at a time in priority order until you have either scheduled all of your activities or you have run out of time spaces.

A good idea here, if it seems you'll run out of time spaces, is to start scheduling the most important activities first. For instance, consider the following activity: "Complete readings and review notes." This activity might take 3 hours and could be placed almost anywhere in the week where you have time and where you'll likely be able to work.

You might schedule three one-hour blocks, two 90-minute blocks or one three-hour block, depending on your preferences. The key here is to associate the specific task to specific times, avoiding making a schedule where the tasks are too closely scheduled or where important activities are assigned to unrealistic work times.

Construct a plan for each week, following the rhythm of your courses that meet weekly. To help make planning a routine activity, pick a regular day each week to schedule. Even with unexpected occurrences that can impact your schedule you assist yourself in making decisions that are governed by your desire to reach your goals.

Without using a schedule you may be governed by your moment-to-moment moods which may lead you to make time decisions that take you away from your goals. Once your week is planned you will experience clarity of focus, your tendency to be distracted will be reduced and you will be certain of your reasons for doing the things you had planned. Committing yourself to a plan you've made represents a renewal of your motivation for the goals and tends to increase your time on task.

Another valuable tool you might want to consider is the dry erase board. Hang this over your computer or study area so it is always visible. Write down important dates like that Microeconomics exam, when your English paper is due, and the big party next weekend. Keeping yourself updated at a glance will help to keep you on tasks as you focus on the reward of studying – that big party next weekend!

Now that you have these valuable tools in your planners, the next step is maximizing on the time you have available.

TIME MANAGEMENT 101

The time you spend on task has some relationship to the quality of work you end up producing. A good gauge to follow is to perform 2-3 hours of schoolwork outside class for every hour of class time. Yes, this means for a full-time student with 15-hours of class per week load the recommendation is to do between 30 and 45 hours of homework each week.

Sure, that's a big jump, especially if you breezed through high school or previous years of college on less. This estimate simply reflects the time it actually takes to learn effectively. It's not steadfast and set in stone. If you find yourself really grasping the concepts of a chapter after a half-hour, feel free to stop. The key here is to set aside this time exclusively for studying. If you get done earlier than expected – that's a bonus!

Now this number shouldn't mean that you completely forgo time for yourself. It is important to have some personal time. Even though you may work a part-time job, and doing so isn't necessarily counter-productive to success at school, you'll need to take some time for yourself and for recreation each week.

A starting guideline might be something like 10% of your week, or 17 hours. What is more important than these specific targets is that you spend enough time on school work to ensure that you're successful and that you spend enough time outside of school to ensure that you have a healthy balance.

Allow for unanticipated interruptions in your schedule. This means leaving some empty spaces during the day or in some way being flexible enough to handle interruptions. If the unexpected does not happen, time is available to do something we were saving until the next day.

Schedule homework early in the day so it is less likely to be crowded out by unexpected events like meeting an old friend or having a roommate ask for help with one of his classes. Homework should be a part of each day's schedule. Students who participated in a major study on stress, reported doing homework as the most frequently used method for reducing stress in their lives.

That might sound odd to you, but by staying ahead of the game and keeping homework done, the stress levels will be lower because you won't have that unfinished work hanging over your head and in your mind constantly.

Remember again that your daily schedule should include at least some time for doing what we want to do rather than just a long list of "have-to-dos." Looking forward to something each day is good for our mental health and can help prevent the feeling of burnout.

Some days may feel overwhelming when we look at our schedule. If this is the case, it is helpful to concentrate on one thing at a time and avoid looking at the whole day. We will be amazed how quickly the tasks of the day will be completed.

Inevitably, you will need to make adjustments to your plans and your time management habits. As you encounter time troubles, keep in mind that some are predictable, some are not; some are controllable, some are not. For those that are not controllable, keep your cool and get back on track as soon as possible. For time troubles that you can control, and particularly those that occur predictably, deal with them directly and forcefully so that they don't prevent you from achieving your goals.

Time management requires self-management. It takes time but after a short period of self-management, time-management becomes an everyday habit.

- Pay attention to how your time is spent.

- Do not procrastinate on chores to be done. Do not leave assignments and projects until the last minute.

- Schedule enough time in the day for doing things you enjoy and for eating and sleeping. Getting enough sleep is beneficial to those with an active schedule.
- Learn to delegate things that do not need your attention.

- Use your time wisely. If you take the bus, plan to catch up on your reading while traveling.

Possibly one of the best time management strategies is staying one day ahead. I'm sure this statement is met by some collective groans, but I promise that staying exactly one day ahead of your classes will make your life much easier.

At the beginning of most of your classes, your professors probably will give you one of the most important pieces of information you will ever receive -- the syllabus. In high school you probably never received a syllabus. You didn't know what the reading assignment or homework assignment was going to be in two weeks. In college, if the syllabus is any good, you do. Why is this important? It is the key to taking control of your time.

Let's say it's the very first day of class. You get your syllabus for your biology class. In most cases, the first day of class is a no-brainer -- often lecture doesn't really begin because the professor knows that a lot of people are going to do the "schedule shuffle." You eye your nifty syllabus and see that the next class period will be a lecture over the first chapter of your $189.99 book. At this critical juncture, you may think:

"Wow, I already know what I'll be doing next class period. I wonder if this is really valuable information? Could I use this to my advantage?"

Needless to say, many people ignore this golden syllabus, stuff it into their pocket, make a paper airplane, or find some other creative use for this sheet of paper and do nothing until next class period.

So next class period arrives two days later, you haven't read chapter one, but who cares, because your professor is going to talk about it. You figure that you will use the time-honored tradition of taking notes in class. After all, everyone's doing it...

But if you're spending all of your time trying to copy overheads or copy written words (your professor will most likely have handwriting that resembles some ancient language), you simply aren't going to really absorb the material in most cases.

Let's say you take some great notes - good for you! Then you take the notes, which have all of the information you will ever need, and you put them in your folder, binder, backpack, or saddle-pack and leave them there until next lecture. Then you take more notes, add them to the pile, and soon you have lots of notes. Whoopee.

Before you know it, you have a test or quiz approaching, so you assemble your nifty notes and start restudying them like mad. You have to set apart a large chunk of time out of your schedule to review this old information so that you will be fresh for your test. There is a better way.

Now, let's pretend that you decided to get one day ahead. After your first class period (and I know this is hard to do because during the first week there's so much fun to be found and so little work to do), you have a heart-to-heart with yourself and decide that you are going to get one day ahead.

If today's Monday, and next class is Wednesday, you set aside some time on Monday afternoon or anytime on Tuesday and read the first chapter. You may even decide to take your own notes, highlight, or even make flashcards for definitions (more on flashcards later).

So when you walk into class on Wednesday and your teacher starts talking, you have at least some idea what they are talking about. You don't have to copy down definitions you've already read off sloppy overheads because you know they are in the book -- you remember reading them. Instead of frantically trying to copy notes like your poor, confused classmates, you can relax a little and really listen to what the professor is saying.

Lecture becomes your own review session, and then you are that much ahead when test time comes. If the professor starts talking about something that you don't remember make certain to take good notes. The topic is either not covered in the book (so you can guarantee the professor will put it on a test), or it's something that you didn't quite absorb the first time you read it.

If you can do this for each of your classes at the very beginning of school, you will be in pristine shape. Once you get one day ahead, you can work at the same pace as everyone else, but always be a day ahead. Lectures will not be "note cramming sessions"; they'll be pseudo reviews.

The toughest part is not getting lazy by using that one day as a buffer. You can't let yourself slip behind because you know you're that much ahead already. Once you lose that day, it's much, much harder to get it back in the middle of the semester because the pace of your classes will be picking up. If you can get ahead in that first week, the load will be much lighter.

Of course, there are exceptions to every rule. Not every class is equal in difficulty, and it may be extremely hard to get that one-day edge in certain classes that have very poor books, or in classes that depend almost 100% on lecture material that doesn't come from your book.

Some classes may be just plain hard, and if you can't get a day ahead in one or two classes, that's fine. The time that you save by being ahead in your other classes will help you enormously in that really tough Microeconomics class you're taking.

If you find that reading your book is doing you no good, then go talk to your professor. If they learn that you are really trying to stay a day ahead, besides the inevitable brownie points that will follow, they will be willing to help you out. Professors are generally willing to bend over backwards for any student that is putting out a serious effort to succeed in their class.

Let me mention that you may have some classes in which the professor has put together a "notes packet" that really does contain copies of all the overheads and notes that will be used. This could be a trap. Don't let those notes become an excuse to get lazy. Don't think that lecture really doesn't matter because you have all of the material -- get one day ahead in the class notes, and again, all of the lectures will be your own personal review sessions.

All of this does not guarantee your success at college. That's because everyone learns differently. Try some of these suggestions and see if it doesn't leave you with more time than you would have if you tried cram sessions, group study sessions, yoga, or any other technique.

Time management is so much easier when you have control over the other parts of your life. A key concept that goes along with this is organization skills. When you are organized, it's easier to stay on task and reduces your stress.

NOW WHERE DID I PUT THAT?

Generally, college students aren't fully prepared to organize the "stuff" in their lives. Dorm rooms can quickly get over-run with clothes, books, computers, CD's, DVD's, television sets, completed papers, half-completed papers, and the other effects of the college student's life.

Maybe you're still living at home in the same room you've been in since you were a child. You still need to make room for the new trappings of college life. Or if you're a non-traditional student, trying to merge college supplies in with children's toys and pots and pans can be overwhelming. Try a few of these great organization tips.

If you want to effectively use your time, designate certain spaces for certain things. You have the tools – desk, dresser, bookshelf. What you need from the store is a few supplies. Colored file folders, a portable plastic file holder, a penholder, some colored binders, a 3-hole punch, and a few small bins should get you started. You can alter your plan – and probably will – as you decide exactly what is right for you and what works best.

Designate one color for each class and store pending assignments in them as you work on them. Place these folders inside the plastic holder. Be sure to write on the tab which class each is for to ease identification. You can also use the file folder approach to store important papers and receipts. If the bursar needs to see your birth certificate, you want to make sure you can get hold of it quickly.

The colored binders are used for each class to store all papers you receive in that class. As we talked about earlier, you will get a syllabus – put this in the front. Then, whenever you get a handout from your professor, punch it and place it in the binder. Use section dividers to label what information is contained in which section. You should also keep completed assignments in this binder for easy referral and in case your instructor "loses" one of your grades – then you can prove you did the work!

Keep on hand an ample supply of pens and use the bins for small items you accumulate like paper clips, push pins for a bulletin board, stapler, etc. If you have a computer, place all these items within easy reach. Make this your "center of action" and use this space to complete all your work. It's a good idea to keep extra of supplies like floppies, CD-RWs, paper, and printer cartridges – just in case!

Now that you have the tools, let's look at how to keep control. Assignments can disappear in pile of paper. Textbooks can get lost within a mound of laundry. A cluttered college student can even lose their mind! Clutter is something that can pile up anywhere, even in the most scholarly of places, like a college campus. But, there is an answer to this disorder disaster.

The paperwork rule is very simple. There are only three things you can do with paperwork:

1. Act on it
2. File it
3. Toss it

For example, if you get a piece of mail, open it. That is actually one huge clutter problem for some- unopened mail that piles up. After it is opened, you must decide what to do with it. If it is a catalog or a piece of junk mail and you know that you are not going to use, toss it. If it is a bill, write it out and mail it, or file it in a "bills due" folder. If you receive a memo or note, after reading it, toss it or file it away. If you get a paper back, file it away. If you don't, this is how stuff clutters on our desks.

Another important place to de-clutter is your computer. If you can keep your files under control, you won't be looking in 20 different folders in "My Documents" for that English paper you wrote last week. Here are some suggestions to get rid of computer clutter.

- Delete e-mail that was already read. This will keep your inbox clean.

- Reply to e-mail right away, so that your inbox does not get built up.

- Create a filing system- if you cannot reply right away, or need to save an e-mail, place in a folder made for that category. (Needs Reply, or Archives)

- Watch your "sent mail" folder. Delete things from that as well. Be sure to delete anything unnecessary from there.

- Add to your address book often. Many times people will keep an e-mail in their inbox so that they have the address when ready to write back. Instead of that, simply save the address. You'll know where to find it later.

- Put spam filters on your e-mail account to limit inbox space. Just don't forget to check your junk mail folder for things to slip through.

- Keep a disk or CD with your assignments from previous classes. This will keep your "My Documents" folder easier to navigate through, as well as allow for more space. In addition, you will have things backed up in case of failure.

Organization is a skill that can be learned. The most difficult part is breaking your lifelong bad habits (like letting your paperwork pile up). The key to getting better organized is to start with one small step and then take others one at a time. You may find that what you've put off for years takes only an hour to do. And once you see the benefits in one part of your life, you'll be motivated to go on.

All the time management and organization tips in the world can only help if you put them to use. Putting things off can be the biggest mistake most college students make.

I'LL STOP PROCRASTINATING TOMORROW

Procrastination is a schedule buster. It's easy to put things off until later, especially when you dread the task such as writing a term paper. But in college, this is a real problem. If you put off your assignments or studying for tests, you are only hurting yourself. Procrastinating leads to stress and anxiety not to mention poor performance. You CAN stop procrastination from affecting your schoolwork.

It can be difficult to start working. Most of the time, however, not starting seems to be related to fear of poor results or negative evaluations than it is to the actual difficulty of the work. Aim to subdivide tasks into small steps and convince yourself that to get started all you need is 10 full minutes working on a task. Often, the 10 minutes will elapse and you'll be right into the swing of things, prepared to continue on productively.

Sometimes you just don't feel motivated to do your schoolwork. It might help to realize that for many people motivation isn't a prerequisite to action...it is a result of it! Try working for a short time and see if you can "get into it."

If your motivation problem seems more substantial, it might help to realize that when you aren't motivated to do school work, you aren't actually out of motivation...you're just motivated to do something else.

Make a schedule. Allocate specific times to complete tasks using daily planners. We have a whole chapter on that in this book. Your planner should always be handy and you should refer to it often. Once you make your schedule, follow it. Work with a roommate or friend to motivate each other. Remember always that once the work is done, you will have more time for yourself, so stick with that schedule.

Make two activity lists: "Things I Like To Do" and "Things I Have To Do". Mix up activities from both lists and work on each activity for a short period of time. Alternating between fun and work helps to maintain motivation and interest. All work and no fun is another schedule buster. You don't have to be working ALL the time, but you do have to complete what needs to be done.

Sometimes, you may feel overwhelmed with large projects. This is a normal reaction. When you feel like this, it's easier to put it off because you don't know exactly where to start and have a difficult time envisioning the completed task. Divide these major assignments into smaller parts and work on one part at a time. Then put them together into the whole project and feel the satisfaction of a job well done!

Some people procrastinate because they have too much to do. You might have every intention of doing things in a timely manner, but time can move swiftly. There are only 24 hours in a day. Thoughtfully examine your obligations and responsibilities. Make sure your schedule is realistic and you aren't involved in too many activities at one time. If you spread yourself too thinly, none of your projects will get the attention they deserve.

Some people are good at summarizing major ideas. Others write exceptionally well. Some people work well with others. Find out what your assets are. Then work them into everything you do. This will improve your confidence and motivation for tackling a distasteful job.

Reward yourself lavishly when tasks are completed on time. Make the reward appropriate for the difficulty and boredom of the task.

Remember that you're not alone. Some studies report that up to 40% of college students experience procrastination as a real problem. Many students tend to mass their practice. That is, do most of the work in marathon sessions near academic deadlines and fail to make appropriate use of various study aids and supports at appropriate times. Doing this only leads to more stress in your already stressful life. Why add to it?

But why do you procrastinate on tasks related to goals you want to achieve? Procrastination often emerges as a means of distancing oneself from stressful activities. People allocate more time to the judged-easy task than to judged-difficult tasks. Dealing with the underlying stressful aspects of the activities can assist in reducing the extent of procrastination. We'll address the problem of stress management a little later.

Here's one practical application. If the volume of work on your to-do list overwhelms you, you might benefit from making a "one-item list": re-write the top item from your list at the top of a blank page and work the task to completion, then repeat.

Some people have to overcome procrastination gradually. Studying, like drinking, is usually in binges. Almost no one has trouble studying (a little) the night before a big exam. But without the pressure of an exam, many students find it easy to forget studying.

I'd suggest breaking big jobs down into manageable tasks and working on "getting started," perhaps by tricking yourself by saying "I'll just do five minutes" and then finding out you don't mind working longer than five minutes. This is called the "five minute plan."

The key is to learn the habit of getting started on a task early, i.e. the procrastinator needs to learn to initiate well in advance studying and preparing for papers and exams. Practice starting studying several times every day. As with exercising, getting in control of starting and making it a routine are the secrets.

Other valuable suggestions include:

- Recognize self-defeating problems such as; fear and anxiety, difficulty concentrating, poor time management, indecisiveness and perfectionism.

- Keep your goals in mind and identify your strengths and weaknesses, values and priorities.

- Compare your actions with the values you feel you have. Are your values consistent with your actions?

- Discipline yourself to use time wisely: Set priorities.

- Study in small blocks instead of long time periods. For example, you will accomplish more if you study/work in 60 minute blocks and take frequent 10 minute breaks in between, than if you study/work for 2-3 hours straight, with no breaks. Reward yourself after you complete a task.

- Motivate yourself to study: Dwell on success, not on failure. Try to study in small groups. Break large assignments into small tasks. Keep a reminder schedule and checklist.

- Set realistic goals.

- Modify your environment: Eliminate or minimize noise/distraction. Ensure adequate lighting. Have necessary equipment at hand. Don't waste time going back and forth to get things. Don't get too comfortable when studying. A desk and straight-backed chair is usually best (a bed is no place to study). Be neat! Take a few minutes to straighten your desk. This can help to reduce daydreaming.

- Decide you've had enough, and it's time for change.

- Think about the activities that you use to procrastinate (email, TV, etc.) and set clear time limits on them.

- Set clear goals for each day (e.g., start CHEM problem set, do POL reading, go to friend's recital) and stick to them. Then when you are done, you are free to do whatever you like.

- Break large projects into smaller pieces.

- Remember that procrastination is usually followed by serious academic stress.

- Recall how awful it is to stay up all night to write a paper. That can help you get started on the next one.

- Know that overcoming procrastination is sometimes easier if you talk out strategies for change with someone else.

Balancing classes, homework, working, and fun can lead to a great deal of stress for the average college student. It's normal to feel stressed with so much going on. You may feel like your life has spiraled out of control, but rest assured, your fellow students are feeling somewhat the same way. In the next section, we'll explore stress, what causes it, and how to lessen it.

AAAAAHHHHHH!

College life is full of new experiences and anxieties. It can be the best of times and the worst of times. Meeting new people, learning, and being on your own are the best. Falling behind in class, pulling "all-nighters and final exams can be the worst.

Sometimes the best of times lead to the worst of times. Students who spend too much time meeting new people and "socializing" find themselves skipping class, falling behind in assignments, and "bombing" exams.

Stress is a common and natural condition of our mortal existence. It arises through our daily efforts to achieve goals, relate with others, and adjust to the demands of living in an ever-changing world.

We often view stress as a negative element in our lives and seek to reduce or eliminate it. We forget that there can be a great deal of growth from learning how to deal with stressful situations. Our aim shouldn't be to completely avoid stress, which at any rate would be impossible, but to learn how to recognize our typical response to stress and then try to adjust our lives in accordance with it.

College is a particularly stressful time for most of us with the pressures of examinations, large amounts of reading, research papers, competition for grades, financial expenses, and social and career decisions. Students can effectively deal with stress rather than become discouraged and immobilized by it.

Each of us functions best at a particular stress level. When stress increases beyond that level, the effectiveness of our performance begins to drop. When we pass our peak of effectiveness we usually experience symptoms like forgetfulness, dulled senses, poor concentration, headaches, digestive upsets, restlessness, irritability and anxiety. The occurrence of these symptoms can alert us to take steps to reduce our stress so our effectiveness can remain at a high level.

Some people have a "race horse" life-style and seem to thrive on intense activity while others prefer a "turtle" life-style and function best when their activity level is not intense. Trying to adopt a "turtle" life-style when we really prefer a "race horse" life-style, or vice-a-versa, can be stressful.

We need to trust ourselves as the authority on what is best for us. We should avoid comparing ourselves with others who seem to function with a higher degree of stress in their lives than we do. For example, we should register for the number of credit hours we think we can effectively handle even though our friends may register for more hours. Also, we should get the number of hours of sleep we need even though our roommates may function on fewer hours.

Here are several ideas that will help in your college stress reduction program.

First, and foremost, is getting enough rest. The basic health guideline for sleep is 7-8 hours per night. Unfortunately, the average college student sleeps significantly less than that. Some student health surveys indicate that most college students sleep less than 6 hours and many less than 4 hours per night. And, you know you can't "pay it back." If you average 4-6 hours during the week, you can't sleep 12 on Saturday and pay it back. In fact, sleeping more than 8 hours can make you feel more tired.

Another stress management health tip is to eat regularly. Many college students skip breakfast, or maybe go all day without eating. When your body is deprived of regular energy, it makes up for it by lowering your metabolism, or energy level. In other words, skipping meals does not help you lose weight or stay awake. In fact, it has the reverse affect.

The "quality" of food is also important. Snack foods (chips, candy, fast foods, etc.) aren't necessarily the most healthy. High salt foods can cause excess water retention and eventually lead to high blood pressure. High sugar foods can cause low blood sugar, or hypoglycemia; which is associated with dizziness, tiredness, and fatigue. Well-balanced meals (like mom makes) and nutritious snacks, such as fruit, popcorn, and bagels are recommended.

Regular exercise is a necessary part of your stress ease program. Sports, games, and daily physical activity are essential in helping you stay focused and sharp. Daily exercise breaks during finals week are a must, even if you're just taking a walk around campus to get away from the study area for a few minutes.

Avoid or moderate all substance use. Alcohol and caffeine are the most widely used and abused substances by college students. Alcohol use certainly does not contribute to your ability to study and retain information.

If you are going to drink alcohol (and you are of legal age), do so with a certain degree of intelligence. Drink only moderate amounts. Make sure you have a non-drinking designated driver. And, curtail your alcohol use a few days prior to major exams or projects. There's no better recipe for failure than a hangover and a chemistry final to turn you into a college drop out.

Caffeine is widely used, especially around exam time. A pot of coffee and an "all-nighter" is still a fact of life at most colleges. But excess amounts of caffeine can lead to nervousness and forgetfulness. These are not traits that you would normally like to possess during an exam.

Remember to take time for yourself. Play a video game, watch a movie, talk with friends. If you're feeling overwhelmed and totally stressed out, sometimes all you need is time away to relax and re-group.

"Attitude is everything." What does that mean? The way you think about things can make all the difference in how you react to events. Have you ever noticed how the exact same situation can stress one person out, while it might not affect another person at all? This difference can usually be explained by the way that each individual thinks about the situation. Changing the way you think (a.k.a. cognitive restructuring) can help you manage stressors in your life. Here's how.

Each time something happens in our lives, the information about that event enters our minds. We then interpret it; we form beliefs about what the event means, why it happened or how it is going to affect us. While we can't always control the events that happen, we can control what we think about the event, which in turn shape our feelings about them.

Self-talk is an ongoing internal dialogue we each have. Oftentimes this conversation is overly critical, irrational and destructive. To reduce stress, instead of being your own worst critic, treat yourself with a gentle touch. Talk to yourself like you would a child who you care about very much.

Think about a stressful situation you experienced recently. Come up with both negative/irrational and productive/rational self-talk for the situation.

Example 1:

Situation: I have a huge paper due in two days.
Irrational self-talk: I'll never get it done. Why did I take that stupid class in the first place?
Rational self-talk: I've worked well under pressure in the past. I know I can do it again!

Example 2:

Situation: I came home to discover my roommate left the kitchen a mess.
Irrational self-talk: She is so disrespectful of me. Can't she think about anyone but herself?
Rational self-talk: I know my roommate has a lot going on. She would have cleaned up if she had time.

Remember that you decide which self-talk you choose to listen to. Try to monitor your self-talk and replace negative messages with constructive, rational ones.

There are also a number of relaxation techniques that can help you manage stress and also improve your concentration, productivity and overall well being.

TO GET STARTED

- Find a quiet, relaxing place, where you will be alone for 10-20 minutes to do these exercises. The techniques work best if there are no distractions.

- Practice once or twice a day.

- Stick with the technique that works best for you. Not every technique will work for every person.

- Keep trying. Don't worry if you don't notice a major change immediately. You may need to practice for a few weeks before you begin to feel the benefits.

- Try one or more of the techniques described below.

PROGRESSIVE MUSCLE RELAXATION

This technique can help you relax the major muscle groups in your body. And, it's easy to do.

1. Wear loose, comfortable clothing. Sit in a favorite chair or lie down

2. Begin with your facial muscles. Frown hard for 5-10 seconds and then relax all your muscles.

3. Work other facial muscles by scrunching your face up or knitting your eyebrows for 5-10 seconds. Release. You should feel a noticeable difference between the tense and relaxed muscles.

4. Move on to your jaw. Then, move on to other muscle groups – shoulders, arms, chest, legs, etc. – until you've tensed and relaxed individual muscle groups throughout your whole body.

MEDITATION

This is the process of focusing on a single word or object to clear your mind. As a result, you feel calm and refreshed.

1. Wear loose, comfortable clothing. Sit or lie in a relaxing position.

2. Close your eyes and concentrate on a calming thought, word or object.

3. You may find that other thoughts pop into your mind. Don't worry, this is normal. Try not to dwell on them. Just keep focusing on your image or sound.

4. If you're having trouble, try repeating a word or sound over and over. (Some people find it helpful to play soothing music while meditating.

5. Gradually, you'll begin to feel more and more relaxed.

VISUALIZATION

This technique uses your imagination, a great resource when it comes to reducing stress.

1. Sit or lie down in a comfortable position.

2. Imagine a pleasant, peaceful scene, such as a lush forest or a sandy beach. Picture yourself in this setting.

3. Focus on the scene for a set amount of time (any amount of time you are comfortable with), then gradually return to the present.

DEEP BREATHING

One of the easiest ways to relieve tension is deep breathing.

1. Lie on your back with a pillow under your head. Bend your knees (or put a pillow under them) to relax your stomach.

2. Put one hand on your stomach, just below your rib cage.

3. Slowly breathe in through your nose. Your stomach should feel like it's rising.

4. Exhale slowly through your mouth, emptying your lungs completely and letting your stomach fall.

5. Repeat several times until you feel calm and relaxed. Practice daily.

Once you are able to do this easily, you can practice this technique almost anywhere, at any time.

A major source of stress is people's efforts to control events or other people over whom they have little or no power. When confronted with a stressful situation, ask yourself: is this my problem? If it isn't, leave it alone. If it is, can you resolve it now? Once the problem is settled, leave it alone. Don't agonize over the decision, and try to accept situations you cannot change.

There are many circumstances in life beyond your control, starting with the weather and including in particular the behavior of others. Consider the fact that we live in an imperfect world. Know your limits. If a problem is beyond your control and cannot be changed at the moment, don't fight the situation. Learn to accept what is, for now, until such time when you can change things.

The mantra to keep in mind is three little words – Let It Go. If you can change something, then change it. If you can't, Let It Go. Once you put this into practice, you'll be surprised at how much stress is lifted from your shoulders. When we dwell on situations we cannot change, that's when stress is emphasized. So if you can't do anything about it, Let It Go!

Be mindful that excessive stress can lead to depression. Warning signs include:

- Sadness, anxiety, or "empty" feelings

- Decreased energy, fatigue, being "slowed down"

- Loss of interest or pleasure in usual activities

- Sleep disturbances (insomnia, oversleeping, or waking much earlier than usual)

- Appetite and weight changes (either loss or gain)

- Feelings of hopelessness, guilt, and worthlessness

- Thoughts of death or suicide, or suicide attempts

- Difficulty concentrating, making decisions, or remembering

- Irritability or excessive crying

- Chronic aches and pains not explained by another physical condition

If you find yourself experiencing any of the symptoms listed above for a prolonged period of time – seek help! Most campuses have resources available such as counseling to help stressed-out and depressed college students cope. Don't let yourself believe that "it's just the blues". Sometimes feeling down can spiral out of control. There are many medications and solutions available to treat depression and make the sun shine again!

It is easy to fall into a "rut" of seeing only the negative when you are stressed. Some people have spent years "turning gold into garbage - the Midas touch in reverse."

When someone says "That's a nice outfit" the "garbage collector" questions whether that person "really means it." Your thoughts can become like a pair of very dark glasses, allowing little light or joy into your life. What would happen if each day for the next three days, you committed yourself to actively collecting (noticing) five "pieces of gold" from your environment?

Pieces of gold are positive or enjoyable moments or interactions. These may seem like small events but as these "pieces of gold" accumulate they can often provide a big lift to energy and spirits and help you begin to see things in a new, more balanced way – on the road to a less stressful life!

Each day find twenty minutes of 'alone time' to relax. Take a walk, write in a journal or meditate. Don't sweat the small stuff...always ask yourself if the issue at hand is worth getting upset about. If it isn't affecting your goal achievement, it may not be worth fretting over.

Humor and positive thinking are important tools in stress management. Most importantly, communicate! Talking to a person who you trust be they a friend, roommate, family member, professor, significant other or co-worker about issues of concern is helpful. We all need someone to listen

A huge part of taking control of your stress is to tackle it before it happens. Good study habits are important for effective time management. You may have been studying your whole academic life, but in college, things are different. Effective studying leads to an overall positive experience in your classes.

STOP THE CRAMMING!

Many college students don't dedicate the right amount of time toward maximizing their studying. As we mentioned before, cramming and pulling "all-nighters" is still a fact of life on most college campuses. These types of sessions increase stress levels and don't always lead to the best performances.

Learning how to study can be the best way to manage your time and leave a little left over for some parties and/or relaxation. Here are some tips to consider:

1. Identify your "Best Time" for Studying: Everyone has high and low periods of attention and concentration. Are you a "morning person" or a "night person"? Use your power times to study; use the down times for routines such as laundry and errands.

2. Study Difficult Subjects First: When you are fresh, you can process information more quickly and save time as a result.

3. Use Distributed Learning and Practice: Study in shorter time blocks with short breaks between. This keeps you from getting fatigued and "wasting time." This type of studying is efficient because while you are taking a break, the brain is still processing the information.

4. Make Sure the Surroundings are Conducive to Studying: This will allow you to reduce distractions which can "waste time." If there are times in the residence halls or your apartment when you know there will be noise and commotion, use that time for mindless tasks.

5. Make Room for Entertainment and Relaxation: College is more than studying. You need to have a social life, yet, you need to have a balance in your life.

6. Make Sure you Have Time to Sleep and Eat Properly: Sleep is often an activity (or lack of activity) that students use as their time management "bank." When they need a few extra hours for studying or socializing, they withdraw a few hours of sleep. Doing this makes the time they spend studying less effective because they will need a couple hours of clock time to get an hour of productive time. This is not a good way to manage yourself in relation to time.

FLASHCARDS

Flashcards are a gift from above to all students who have those classes that seem to revolve around definitions, dates, or memorizing equations. If you're really smart, while reading material, you will take the time to copy definitions or important acts onto a 3" x 5" index card. When you finish the chapter, you should have a little stack of compact information that will prove to be invaluable.

Don't try to copy everything down. Concentrate on the major points that you'll need to remember come test time. The simple act of writing down the information will make your brain start to think about the new information and retain it easier.

When you look back over the cards, you might be surprised that you can remember some of what you just wrote down before even studying it. Keep making cards for the new material you read and/or get in class lecture. When test time comes, you won't have to waste your time going back through notes and books trying to sift the important information away from the filler. You've already assembled all of the material you need to study, and in most cases, it will fit right into your pocket! Sure beats hauling around a textbook!

Sit down two or three days before an exam and go through your flashcards. Try to reproduce all of the definitions – either by saying them out loud or writing them down. Writing takes longer to do, but you will remember them faster if you have to write them in most cases, thus saving you time in the long run.

If you get a card right put a tally mark in the corner. When you have three to five tally marks on a card (depending on how well you think you need to know the material), then you can be pretty certain you know your stuff. Soon the cards you know readily will be marked up with tally marks, and the ones that are tricky will be left. Study these extra hard, and when all of your beautiful flashcards are covered with tally marks, you're finished. Prepare to collect your A.

The night before the test arrives, your companions are sifting through notes, books, copies of overheads, etc., but you calmly reach for your flashcards and review stuff that you already knew two days ago. Maybe you've forgotten some, no problem. Review them a couple more times, slap down some more tally marks when you get them right, and again, you're finished.

And guess what? Eighteen months down the line you're going to have a final. One of the most difficult things about studying for finals is that you have to gather all of the information for the entire semester so that you can study it. Some people spend all week copying old notes, reviewing book material, etc., just to GET READY to study for exams.

But, if you've been making flashcards and keeping them, you should have a convenient little pile of things you should know. You don't have to spend time sifting through an entire semester of information because you've been doing that already, one day at a time. You're ready to study.

Plus, you can have your flashcards with you at all times so you can take advantage of stolen time – waiting in lines, waiting to see the doctor, waiting for your Starbucks. Maximizing down time with flashcards makes tedious studying much, much easier.

Reading that Microeconomics textbook isn't the most interesting thing on your to do list. We know that. There is an effective technique you can use while reading, though, that will help maximize what you get out of the material. It may seem complicated at first, but once you get into the habit of doing it, you'll notice a change in how you study.

This technique is called SQ3R – survey, question, read, recite, review. It is a proven way to sharpen your study skills. Here's how it works:

Survey - get the best overall picture of what you're going to study <u>before</u> you study it in any detail. It's like looking at a road map before going on a trip. If you don't know the territory, studying a map is the best way to begin.

Question - ask questions for learning. The important things to learn are usually answers to questions. Questions should lead to emphasis on the what, why, how, when, who and where of study content.

Ask yourself questions as you read or study. As you answer them, you will help to make sense of the material and remember it more easily because the process will make an impression on you. Those things that make impressions are more meaningful, and therefore more easily remembered. Don't be afraid to write your questions in the margins of textbooks, on lecture notes, or wherever it makes sense.

Read - Reading is NOT running your eyes over a textbook. When you read, read actively. Read to answer questions you have asked yourself or questions the instructor or author has asked. Always be alert to **bold** or *italicized* print. The authors intend that this material receive special emphasis. Also, when you read, be sure to read everything, including tables, graphs and illustrations. Often times tables, graphs and illustrations can convey an idea more powerfully than written text.

Recite - When you recite, you stop reading periodically to recall what you have read. Try to recall main headings, important ideas of concepts presented in bold or italicized type, and what graphs charts or illustrations indicate. Try to develop an overall concept of what you have read in your own words and thoughts. Try to connect things you have just read to things you already know. When you do this periodically, the chances are you will remember much more and be able to recall material for papers, essays and objective tests.

Review - A review is a survey of what you have covered. It is a review of what you are supposed to accomplish not what you are going to do. Rereading is an important part of the review process. Reread with the idea that you are measuring what you have gained from the process.

During review, it's a good time to go over notes you have taken to help clarify points you may have missed or don't understand. The best time to review is when you have just finished studying something. Don't wait until just before an examination to begin the review process. Before an examination, do a final review. If you manage your time, the final review can thought of as a "fine-tuning" of your knowledge of the material.

Learn to keep notes logically and legibly. Remember, if you can't read your own writing a few days after taking notes, they are of little use. By all accounts, the best place to keep notes is in a loose-leaf notebook. Use dividers to separate the different classes you take. Make it a habit of using your notebook to record ALL your notes.

If you're caught without your notebook and need to take notes, always have a supply of loose-leaf paper with you. Insert your notepapers into the notebook as soon as you can. Be sure to buy a good notebook, as it will get a lot of wear and tear.

Now that we've got studying covered, let's look at another huge aspect of college life – paying the bills and finding the money to do so!

WORKIN 9 TO 5

For many college students, having to hold down a part-time or even full-time job is one that is a harsh reality. Not all of us have parents with an endless supply of cash and some of us just choose to earn our own money instead of depending on others. So how do you balance your job with everything else?

Of course, above everything else is scheduling. Be sure your boss knows your class schedule and have a heart-to-heart with him or her about your time needs. Many workplaces are sympathetic to the plight of the working college student. Communication is essential to having a peaceful co-existence with your job and your schooling.

Family-owned businesses tend to be much more understanding of the college student. They have shown to be more willing to work with employees who are full-time students.

Consider finding work on campus. Check the bulletin boards for jobs that will fit into your schedule or find the human resources department and inquire about available positions. Many colleges offer work in your field of study, which could prove to be invaluable. Working on campus eliminates travel time to an outside job and minimizes the stress of trying to coordinate classes with your job.

Don't try to take on too many hours. Studies show that students who work more than 15 hours at a part-time job while carrying a full load of classes experience more stress and have a larger chance of dropping out of school due to that stress. While it's important to have income to offset expenses, it's also important to concentrate on your studies.

Take advantage of downtime. When you have a break, review your flashcards. On your lunch or dinner break, read a chapter while eating a sandwich. Talk to your employer about studying during lulls while on the clock. If you work at, say, a convenience store, see if your boss would be willing to allow you study time in between customers. When you take advantage of the time you're given your success at balancing work and studies will increase greatly.

Working while in college offers the student more than just the chance to make money. College jobs allow students to work with faculty and administrators who can often serve as mentors. And students can often find jobs that relate to their academic work (lab work, research, etc.). Just as importantly, campus jobs often provide students with the opportunity to examine various career options. At the very least, potential employers appreciate the fact that students worked while they were in college.

Don't be afraid to let your professors know that you have a job. Most teachers have learned to turn a deaf ear to students with poor excuses for not doing their assignments on time, but that doesn't mean they aren't willing to make exceptions when they know the need is there. On the other hand, don't allow your friends to think you're never available because of your job. Make a point of putting aside time so that you can take part in at least some of their activities.

Although working while in college is important, it's not for everyone. Working, like the rest of one's college experiences, must be kept in perspective. Working should be a complement rather than a hindrance to the student's academic activities. Try it -- if it doesn't work or if academic problems occur, talk with your academic dean. Immediately!

If working gets to be too much, consider other routes for earning cash, or modify your budget. You should NEVER let work hold you back from achieving your dream of a college education. There are many resources available. Take advantage of them. Use them. Go to the financial aid office and discuss your situation with a counselor there. You might be surprised at the options you will have available.

Consider some of these other tips:

- **Get a work-study job if eligible.** The Federal Work-Study Program offers jobs to eligible Federal financial aid recipients. If you apply for and are awarded with Federal financial aid, your award letters will identify whether or not you are eligible for work-study and the number of hours you will be allowed to work.

If you are eligible, you can then go to your financial aid office and apply for available work-study jobs. These jobs can either be on campus or off campus and are usually at a non-profit organization or public agency. These organizations generally let students work very flexible hours.

- **Get a job that includes tips.** Jobs with wages plus tips pay the best. So, if you are looking to earn a lot of money while in college, consider being a waiter or waitress at a local restaurant. Just keep in mind that these job hours may not be as flexible as a job on campus or a work-study job.

- **Advertise your services.** If you like to type or edit papers or tutor other students, why not get paid for it? Put up posters around campus that show students what you are offering and how much you charge.

No matter what route you take to make more money, try to find one that doesn't interfere too much with your schoolwork. If you are having trouble finding the time to go to class or do your homework, try cutting back on your hours at work. Just keep in mind that eating cans of tuna and Ramen noodles is much better than failing a class.

Another component to reducing stress and maximizing your time is effectively managing your money. Whether it comes from mom and dad or your own hard-earned paycheck, money management for college students is essential to learn.

JUST BECAUSE THERE'S CHECKS STILL IN THE BOOK.....

Money certainly makes the world go 'round, and we all need to be mindful of how much we have and where it's going. This is especially true for college students. College expenses can be high with tuition, books, room and board, rent, gas, beer money, movie rentals, etc. Effective money management is made easier with these tips.

First, track your spending for two to four weeks to find out where your money is going. Is four trips to Starbucks a week really necessary? You probably don't realize how much money you spend on little things like snacks and poker antes. Often, just by tracking expenses, you'll start to curb your expenses and spend your money wisely.

The best way to manage your money over the course of a semester is to sit down and map out a budget. List sources of income such as scholarships, loans, money from summer jobs, and cash from your parents. Then list your expenses, such as tuition, books and groceries. If your income is larger than your outgo, you're on the right track!

If you know you *need* to buy a new CD or go to concert or a party every week, make room for that in your budget. You do need some entertainment. You'll get burned out if you don't have any fun. But be mindful of your entertainment expenses so that they don't get out of hand.

If you spend, spend, spend at the beginning of the semester, you could be tapped out later. Give yourself a spending limit for each week. Stick to it and you won't have to eat macaroni-and-cheese every day in December.

Be careful with credit card use. Having a credit card is a good idea in case of emergencies, but having that little piece of plastic can make your spending get way out of control, very, very quick. One quick way to spend beyond your means is to charge it. Use credit cards sparingly. Once you get into the habit of reaching for a Visa, it can be hard to stop.

Keep only one credit card. You'll probably be barraged with offers from credit card companies wanting to give you a $5,000 credit limit at only 25% interest to celebrate your induction into the "real world". Find a card with a low interest rate and use it as little as possible. And don't charge small purchases! If you need a bag of chips, search the couch cushions for spare change before you plunk down the Master Card. You don't want to be paying interest on a bag of chips!

You can set your own credit limit instead of letting the credit card company set it for you. Just because you have a credit card with a $2,000 credit line doesn't mean you have to spend $2,000. If you know you can only pay back $500, then just spend that.

If you're afraid you'll keep spending as long as there's room on the card? Call your credit card company and request your credit limit be lowered. Keep at it. Card companies will try boost up your credit lines so you spend more. Tell them "no" each time they try.

Be realistic about your spending habits. You can do what you want, but you can't do <u>everything</u> you want. You're going to have to make some choices. Whatever you choose is going to cost some money. You need to understand you can't have everything and you have to understand there's consequences. At some point there needs to be a reality check in terms of what things cost. Most students have no idea.

If you bust your budget on something you really, really want to do this week, make up for it next week. If you find that you must go out to dinner and a movie one week, spend the money; be satisfied with the decision, and commit to staying home, eating at home, and not making any other purchases the following week.

Plan ahead for big expenses. Whether it's a road trip with friends or a car insurance bill, if you know a big expense is coming, start putting some money aside to pay for it. It's a lot easier to set aside $50 every month than to come up with $300 when the bill is due.

When it comes to dorm or apartment expenses, contact your roommate before the semester starts and divvy up expenses. Decide who will bring a refrigerator and who will bring a microwave, etc. This way you avoid duplicating purchases and excess spending but will still have all the conveniences to make college life easier.

Most of the big expenses are at the beginning of the school year. Buy books as you need them. That will spread out expenses. Don't forget to check out prices from online bookstores. They may give you a better deal than the campus bookstore. Buy used books whenever possible. Check e-bay or half.com with the ISBN number of the textbooks you need. You can usually get this number from your college bookstore, and the prices are usually a lot lower than what the bookstore will charge.

Don't forget, too, that when the semester is over, if you have a book you don't think you'll use ever again – Thermonuclear Physics, The History of the Doughnut, etc. – sell them back to the school or list them online. This can be a really easy way to make a little cash at the end of the year.

It's very difficult to say 'I'm in trouble and I need $2,000' or 'I spent my student loan money'. Screw up some courage and phone home. The longer you put it off, the worse things get. While your parents might not be thrilled that you've been so careless with your money, we're willing to bet that they'll probably be ready to help out – after a few moments of lecturing, of course!

Remember that money management is really about resource management. Also, know that money usually operates with us on at least two different levels. There is the practical dimension from which we make purchases. There is also the symbolic level. Money can buy us pleasure, friendships, or give us the feeling of power. We need to be careful not to let money substitute for emotional needs we need to address in other ways.

If money is a little tight, there are some easy things you can do every day to save and avoid the money crunch.

- Don't eat fast food every day. Look into the meal plans offered by the school's cafeteria. Buy quick, convenient things to make in your room like soup or Easy Mac.

- Use coupons for things you frequently buy; keep them in your car so that they are handy for the store, fast food or restaurants

- Rent a movie instead of going out to a theater

- Consolidate errands to cut down on extra gasoline expenses. When you do buy gas, do it in the middle of the week and at a gas station that has competition close by to get the lowest prices.

- Stock up at holiday and back-to-school sales for things you know you will need

- Use email for long distance communication instead of the phone. Consider a new cell phone plan or even switching companies if you can save money by doing so.

- Use a shopping list when at the store; do not deviate from your list whenever possible

- Keep your eye on the register when checking out at stores, purchases can easily be rung up wrong

One final note, as crazy as it may seem, because college is a time of money shortages, consider the idea of putting a little money away on a weekly basis. One dollar a week at the end of the year is still fifty-two dollars. Then do something extraordinarily nice for yourself or with someone else.

Saving is really a part of spending too. See if these brief money-managing tips might not help you achieve your goals and objectives in college. We often say, "If you manage your time, you manage your life. If you waste your time, you waste your life." With money, perhaps we are saying, "Manage it, don't let it manage you."

Now let's move on to the fun stuff – enjoying yourself, making time for fun, and getting the most out of college life!

PARTY RESPONSIBLY

Parties and socializing is a huge part of college life. You should never deny yourself the right to enjoy the non-academic side of the university. You need to keep in mind, however, that partying is only a small part of the college experience. It has its pitfalls, and you need to be careful that you don't overdo it so that it becomes the MOST important part.

When you have an early class, avoid the bars the night before. You're just setting yourself up for trouble. Even if you do get up the next morning after a late night out, you won't be completely focused on the class. This will lead to you missing important information that you might need later on. You won't be performing to your full potential if you're tired or hung over.

Be mindful of the downfalls of excessive alcohol use. We're not saying you have to completely avoid alcohol. If you're of legal age and you want to enjoy a drink or two, by all means, go ahead. But, it's easy for a few drinks to turn into more and before you know it, you've developed a problem. Warning signs that alcohol may be a problem include:

- Missing classes or appointments

- Dropping grades

- Aggressive behavior while drunk

- Erratic behavior while drinking

- Blacking out or poor recollection of events

- Drinking when under stress

If you think you might have a problem, don't hesitate to seek help. Most college campuses have counselors on staff to help with problems affecting college students. Talk to your family doctor or call a help line such as those offered by Alcoholics Anonymous.

Never, ever, drink and drive. Take a cab, take turns with your friends being designated driver, or walk (but be careful – you CAN get a ticket for public intoxication if you're too smashed!) Safety should be first and foremost in your mind – at all costs!

There's much more to college life than partying, though. Enjoy the other aspects of the university. Join an organization you're passionate about. Were you student body president in high school? Look into student council or Young Republicans. If you're interested in acting, consider student theater productions.

Sororities and fraternities are present on most four-year campuses. These are great places to activate new friendships that can last for a lifetime. There's often a "rush" week during which time you can visit the houses and learn more about which groups you might want to be part of.

Often, there is a voting process during which you are accepted or rejected. Don't be discouraged if you aren't accepted into your first choice. They might just think you're not a good fit with their personalities and/or lifestyle. Just don't give up. Being part of a fraternity or sorority can be great fun and a huge learning experience.

Don't discount calm, laid-back activities as well. Simply watching a movie or playing cards with your dorm-mates can be great relaxation and just as fun as going to a bar – but without the hangover!

Having fun is a big part of college life. You deserve to enjoy the whole experience, so be sure and make time for yourself and cultivating friendships and interests.

So what if you're a non-traditional student? Think this advice doesn't apply to you? Let's address that in our next section.

BUT I'M NOT 18 ANYMORE!

More and more mature adults are going back to college to complete degrees already started, to fulfill a lifelong ambition, or to train for a new career path. Time management for non-traditional students is especially crucial as the issue of children and family contributes to the already hectic life of a full-time college student. Some non-traditional students also juggle full-time jobs along with their studies. Finding time to study, take care of a home, work an outside job, and have a personal life seems out of reach. However, time management skills make it not only possible, but also realistic.

Refer to the section in this book regarding using your planner. With other activities going on in your lives, having a planner and referring to it often is more crucial than ever. You will also want to invest in a dry erase board for your home in a calendar format to keep track of events, appointments, and homework assignments. This can be especially helpful so that your family always knows where you are. Keep the board in a convenient, well referred to place such as the refrigerator or by the front door.

Use a different color marker for each family member so you know who is where and when. List your class schedule on the dry erase board and have your family members record their activities along with times to keep track of everyone's schedule. It's a good idea to copy this same schedule down in your planner since your planner should always be with you and you will always know how to schedule your hectic life.

Remember why you are in college in the first place and make this a priority in your life. It's essential that you talk with family and friends to insure they understand that even though they do matter tremendously to you, school has to be important and their support is needed in that.

Allot a specific time each day for studying. You need a quiet place with minimal distractions. You may want to physically write your study schedule on the dry erase board as well. Let your family know that when you're studying, you must be left alone. Then do nothing else during that time. Shut off the phone, stay put, and concentrate on your studies.

Organization is another key component to effective time management. While we do have a whole section in here on organization, some special attention needs to be taken to address your special circumstances. You need to identify one specific place to keep all your books and reference materials. Keep a separate bag or backpack to hold that day's books and anything you will need for class. Always keep an ample supply of pens and extra floppy disks or a jump drive in this bag along with small change for the snack machines.

When you study, designate a separate study space where you can be away from your family. I usually use the dining room table or go to the basement where it's quiet. The key is to eliminate all distractions and focus on your schoolwork. Make sure you keep a supply of paper and pencils nearby this space as well.

Take advantage of "stolen" time. You can study on your lunch break at work, while watching your child's soccer game, sitting in the doctor's office, or anywhere you have waiting time. Of course, in the car on the freeway would probably be a bad idea!

You might be apprehensive and even nervous about returning to school, but realize that this is a normal reaction. You're returning to a setting you haven't seen in awhile, and when you get there, you'll be among much younger people, which can seem overwhelming. Don't feel alone. Look around the campus. I'd bet you're not the only one there.

Chances are, the traditional college student won't really notice or even care that you're older than they are. Once the class is in full swing and you're part of the class environment, you may be surprised when some of those younger students come to you for help and/or advice.

Take advantage of all the resources your college has to offer such as electronic library resources, help centers, and tutors. Don't be afraid to ask for help – especially from your professors. If you do not understand something in the class, arrange a meeting when your professor has office hours. Most instructors are more than willing to help out their students – especially the non-traditional ones!

Almost every college has a program for the non-traditional student that helps with adjusting to college life, honing your study skills, and dealing with the pressures of juggling studies, family, and work. Use these services. They were made for YOU!

YOU CAN DO IT!

Whether you're embarking on your college career just out of high school or later in life, time management and all that goes with it is a very important aspect of a successful college experience. If you control your time, you control your stress, and you perform to the best of your abilities.

There are so many aspects of a college education that rely on positively managing your time, your money, your life. While it might seem overwhelming at first, if you tackle one thing at a time, it will be much more manageable and easier to achieve the goals that you set for yourself.

Keep your eye on the "prize". Never forget why you're in college and remember that with the right tools, you can achieve your dreams. Refer to this book often. It is a gathering of personal experience, time-honored tips from the pros, and practical advice that works.

Before you know it, you'll be walking across that stage again and collecting a diploma – only this time, it will say "College Graduate"

Good luck!

www.ingramcontent.com/pod-product-compliance
Lightning Source LLC
LaVergne TN
LVHW020437080526
838202LV00055B/5241